INTRODUCING

Descartes

Dave Robinson and Chris Garratt

Edited by Richard Appignanesi

ICON BOOKS UK   TOTEM BOOKS USA

This edition published in the UK in 1999 by Icon Books Ltd., Grange Road, Duxford, Cambridge CB2 4QF email: icon@mistral.co.uk www.iconbooks.co.uk

First published in the United States in 1998 by Totem Books Inquiries to: PO Box 223, Canal Street Station, New York, NY 10013

Distributed in the UK, Europe, Canada, South Africa and Asia by the Penguin Group: Penguin Books Ltd., 27 Wrights Lane, London W8 5TZ

In the United States, distributed to the trade by National Book Network Inc., 4720 Boston Way, Lanham, Maryland 20706

This edition published in Australia in 1999 by Allen & Unwin Pty. Ltd., PO Box 8500, 9 Atchison Street, St. Leonards NSW 2065

Library of Congress Catalog Card Number: 97–062432

Previously published in the UK and Australia in 1998 under the title *Descartes for Beginners*

Originating editor: Richard Appignanesi

Printed and bound in Australia by McPherson's Printing Group, Victoria

The Modern Beginner

Everyone agrees that modern philosophy began with Descartes. Why "modern"? Because he insisted on thinking for himself, rather than just accepting what he had been taught. By this method, Descartes believed he could establish the philosophical and mathematical foundations for all of human knowledge – an ambitious quest which eventually turned out to be strangely personal and deeply subjective. Descartes' philosophy is like a spiritual journey which he invites the reader to join, and which he always promised would produce extraordinary results ...

I shall bring to light the true riches of our souls, opening up to each of us the means whereby we can find within ourselves all the knowledge we may need for the conduct of life and the means of using it in order to acquire all the knowledge that the human mind is capable of possessing ...

Early Days and Youth

René Descartes was born in 1596 in La Haye, in the Touraine region of France. (The town is now called *Descartes*!) He was the son of a nobleman, which meant that he never had to work for a living. When he was eight, he was sent to the Jesuit school of La Flèche in Anjou. At this Catholic school he learnt Greek and Latin as well as mathematics and Scholastic philosophy.

At school, I came to the conclusion that mathematics was the only subject of any real worth – a view I held all of my life.

ALMA MATER

His health was poor and so he was granted permission to stay in bed every morning until 11 o'clock – a habit he kept to in adult life. Descartes always set aside a few morning hours for concentrated thought and devoted the rest of the day to rest and relaxation.

Shortly after leaving La Flèche, Descartes wrote a book that no longer survives called **The Art of Fencing**, which gave detailed instructions on the different techniques and strategies necessary to beat your opponent. Descartes was said by some to have been as good a swordsman as he was a philosopher. He would have made an interesting fourth musketeer.

Descartes' first published work was a small treatise on music.

Eventually he went on to study law at the University of Poitiers and, although he qualified as a lawyer, he never practised.

The Soldier

Instead, Descartes decided to travel and see a bit of the world.

I spent my youth travelling, visiting courts and armies, mixing with people of diverse temperaments and ranks.

He was a small man, with a large head, a big nose and a rather feeble voice. Nevertheless, he became a soldier and joined the army of Maurice of Nassau of the Netherlands, and then the German army of Maximilian of Bavaria. The whole of Europe was being torn apart by the conflicts known as the Thirty Years War (1618-48). Descartes wasn't cut out for the military life – he consequently absented himself from war and politics. *"I am a spectator rather than an actor in the comedies of life."*

One reason for this was a chance meeting on 10 November 1618 in the town of Breda in Holland. Descartes had seen a placard written in Dutch and so asked a passing stranger to translate it for him. The stranger was Isaac Beeckman, who soon became a close friend.

Descartes' Three Dreams

On 10 November 1619, Descartes found himself stuck in the small town of Neuburg-on-Danube. He was a rather unenthusiastic soldier of 23 en route to see the coronation of Ferdinand II in Frankfurt. But the Bavarian winter was severe and he had to postpone his journey.

"… the onset of Winter detained me in lodgings where, because there was no conversation to amuse me and happily having no worries or passions to trouble me, I stayed all day shut up alone in a stove-heated room, where I was completely free to commune with myself about my own thoughts."

The First and Second Dreams

The thoughts that Descartes had in this stove-heated room, surrounded by blizzards, changed the whole of Western philosophy for ever. He had the most extraordinary sequence of vivid dreams.

When he awoke he spent the next two hours terrified that this strange vision had been put into his mind by some evil demon.

His next dream wasn't much of an improvement – he heard a huge thunderclap and found himself trapped in a room full of fire and sparks.

The Third Dream

Fortunately, his third dream was quieter. He was looking at several books by the side of his bed. There was an encyclopedia and an anthology of poems …

Descartes had always been interested in mathematics and science, and his last dream told him that there was a way in which all human knowledge could be made into a unified whole. *"If we could see how the sciences linked together, we would find them no harder to retain in our minds than the series of numbers."*

He always believed in his dream and he never gave up the quest it had set him. Because of this odd night in a cold and strange town, Descartes became the most important and influential philosopher of his time.

Descartes Settles in Holland

Between 1619 and 1623, Descartes travelled all over Europe. He claimed that he was almost murdered by some sailors when he was in Friesland, but frightened them off with his sword. In 1623, he visited the shrine of the Virgin at Loretto – to fulfil a vow he'd made after his vivid dreams four years earlier. He then lived in Paris for the next four years. But in 1628 he moved to the Netherlands where he spent the rest of his life. Perhaps he preferred the more tolerant Protestant society of Holland to his own country of France.

I could lead a life as solitary and as withdrawn as if I were in the most remote desert. In what other country could I enjoy such complete freedom?

In 1635 Descartes became a father. He had formed a relationship with his servant Hélène earlier in Amsterdam, and in that year both mother and child came to live with him in his rural retreat near Santpoort. Tragically, his daughter Francine died of scarlet fever when she was only five years old – an event which affected Descartes profoundly. He had no other children.

It was whilst in Holland that Descartes eventually wrote his most famous works: **Philosophical Essays** (1637) (containing the famous **Discourse on the Method**), **Meditations** (1641) and the **Principles of Philosophy** (1644).

Scholasticism

It is important to understand the conditions of philosophy and science that Descartes confronted in his time. When Descartes arrived on the intellectual stage of Europe, the Roman Catholic Church had dominated all intellectual activity for many centuries. Scholars spent their time attempting to integrate the wisdom of ancient classical thinkers like **Aristotle** (384-322 B.C.) with Christian teaching rather than making any attempt to discover new knowledge.

God has given reason to human beings.

So any truths reached by reason must therefore automatically be reconcilable with Christian doctrine.

If any contradictions occur, faith takes precedence over reason. Philosophy is the servant of theology.

This traditional and deeply conservative approach to knowledge is usually known as **Scholasticism**. Scholastic philosophy was essentially a grand metaphysical system of theology concerned with logical deductions from Christian dogma. Its practitioners, known as "schoolmen", were academic philosophers and usually clerics. The most influential Scholastic was the Dominican theologian **St Thomas Aquinas** (1225-74) who became an incontrovertible authority on matters of faith and reason.

The Early Days of Science

Original thought was discouraged and new ideas had to be smuggled in under the guise of commentary on older texts. Because of this profound respect for the past, scholars continued to believe in all of Aristotle's "science", no matter how ridiculous or unbelievable it might be. You found out things by looking through old books rather than telescopes. If Aristotle said that toads could live on air, no one thought it worthwhile to have a look to see if it was true or not.

Scholastics accept Aristotle's unsatisfactorily empty and circular "explanations" for why things behave as they do. According to him, stones fall to the ground because they have a "propensity to fall to the ground".

Descartes was impatient to discover newer and better ways of getting hold of knowledge and truth.

"Knowledge" in Descartes' day was a bizarre mixture of fact and imagination, myth and the occult, religious dogma and wild conjecture. Renaissance "science" still included astrology and alchemy and had an obsession with patterns and resemblances. **Paracelsus** (1493-1541), a Swiss physician who made original and important discoveries in medical treatment, could still think in terms of occult parallels.

Behold the Satyrion root — is it not formed like the male privy parts? Accordingly magic discovered and revealed that it can resolve a man's virility and passion.

The times in which Descartes lived were strangely both medieval and "modern", when "science" as a special and unique kind of human activity was being invented.

In 1627, **Johannes Kepler** (1571-1630) produced accurate predictions of the elliptical orbits of the planets. In Protestant England, **Francis Bacon** (1561-1626) was writing a book about the new power and exciting discoveries produced by "scientific" method. "Modern" scientists like **Galileo Galilei** (1564-1642) were rapidly discovering that a lot of what Aristotle had said was nonsense.

Although many of these new men were "modern" in their attitudes, in other ways they were still very "medieval". None of them ever questioned the existence of God (Descartes frequently invokes and employs God as the guarantor of his philosophical doctrines).

Most of the great scientific thinkers of the 17th century were Christian believers, although this didn't stop them questioning many of the "eternal truths" ruthlessly maintained by the Roman Catholic Church. But in early 17th century Europe it was still dangerous to contradict official Church doctrine and provoke the dreaded Inquisition.

In 1629 Descartes was writing a work on natural phenomena (**The World**) which suggested that the universe might well have the sun at its centre. But in 1633 he heard of Galileo's house-arrest in Italy for suggesting the same thing, and so he wisely postponed publication of his own work.

This has so astonished me that I almost resolved to burn all my papers, or at least not let anyone see them ...

Descartes realized that his new ways of thinking would challenge the powerful academic world of Scholasticism and render it obsolete. But, as he said, *"I desire to live in peace and to continue the life I have begun under the motto – **Keep out of the public eye if you wish to live a happy existence**."*

What is Science?

Descartes believed that there could be a new kind of systematic "scientific" procedure. He tried to explain this by comparing knowledge to a tree.

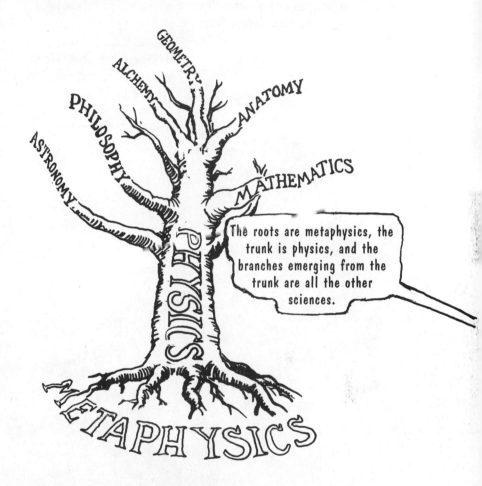

Descartes was groping towards the kind of human activity we now call "science". This is why some of the key words used by Descartes are confusing for modern readers. The words "science" and "philosophy" are often indistinguishable and can mean all kinds of knowledge that we nowadays would no longer call "scientific". He did not make the same kinds of rigid distinctions that we now do between philosophy and science.

Reduction to Mathematics

Descartes hoped to show that there was an underlying unity to all the different branches of knowledge. But what was this unity? There was a growing belief amongst astronomers and scientists that mathematics or direct observation rather than Aristotle or the Bible might be the keys to understanding what the universe was like.

Mathematics expresses the basic fundamental structure shared by all branches of knowledge.

This is one of the main features of modern science, known as **Reductionism**. Numerous kinds of things are reduced and so explained in terms of a much smaller number of basic features or "simple natures" of reality.

Descartes the Scientist

Descartes was himself something of a scientist, although not a very successful or influential one. Some of his science still makes sense. He was the first person to publish the fundamental laws of reflection in optics (that the angle of incidence is equal to the angle of reflection). But a lot of it now seems very odd. Descartes believed that all matter was made up of tiny and infinitely divisible "corpuscles". For him, all matter was "extension" (with length, breadth and height) and all extension matter – so the existence of a vacuum or atoms was just not possible.

R

We know there can be no indivisible atoms ... for if there were such things they would have to be extended, however small, and so divisible ...

And because he had no coherent theory of gravity, the Cartesian universe was made up of swirling vortices – rather like whirlpools of matter. It was a model of the universe accepted until ruthlessly demolished by **Isaac Newton** (1642-1727). Descartes also established the influential idea of primary and secondary qualities.

Cause

Descartes' contribution to the physical sciences is probably more conceptual than practical because he helped to change the way in which scientists think about "cause". Scholastic science maintained that everything had a "final cause" and that this explained how and why it behaved as it did.

Every single thing in the universe is heading towards some final cosmic destination, and it is the scientist's job to find out what this goal is.

DR. SUBTILIS
ARISTOTELIAN
SCHOLAR
1273 – 1308

For me, the "final causes" of things and events are a mystery that perhaps only God knows. The scientist's job is to investigate only those causes that are prior to effects and not to speculate on occult powers or ultimate purposes.

The Aristotelian view of the universe is almost animistic – magnets attract iron because of their "magnetic qualities". Descartes was unimpressed by such unsatisfactory and circular explanations. His universe is mathematical and mechanistic, and so, predictable.

23

Discourse on The Method

Descartes' **Essays** of 1637 are about Optics, Meteorology and Geometry. But it is the Introduction to the essays which is now the most important – the **Discourse on the Method of Rightly Conducting One's Reason and Seeking the Truth in the Sciences**. (A development of an earlier unpublished work, **Rules for the Direction of the Mind**, written in 1628.) Descartes thought that there must be a "method" that would organize the human search for knowledge so that it could become more systematic and successful. **Discourse on the Method** carefully itemizes all the "Rules for the Direction of the Mind" that need to be followed if scientific investigation is to be more than a haphazard mixture of intuition and guesswork. This is where Descartes attempts to show how it is possible to discover true knowledge just by using a few central procedural rules.

You accept only that which is clear to your mind.

You split large problems into smaller ones.

You argue from the simple to the complex.

And finally you check everything carefully when you have finished.

He thought that these rules could be the basis for a new kind of scientific logic.

Clear in the Mind

One rule that Descartes stresses repeatedly is that **true** ideas must be "clear and distinct" in your mind. By "clear", Descartes means that ideas in the mind must be as obvious and apparent to us as physical objects that we see with our eyes.

I call a perception distinct if it is not only clear but also precisely distinguished from all others, so that it contains no element that is not clear.

This kind of *mental* visual clarity makes sense when we are doing geometry or mathematics. We see numbers and geometric figures in our mind and we don't confuse one with another. And, if we have properly understood what we are doing, then our mathematics or geometry will be correct.

What Is a Clear Idea?

But if we apply this "clarity rule" to other kinds of knowledge it seems more ambiguous and less helpful. We may have clear and distinct ideas about all sorts of things – like the earth being flat or the sun moving – but this offers us no guarantee that we are right. The problem with a lot of scientific truths is that they are often *counter-intuitive*. This means that science often goes against the deductions or intuitions of common sense.

Descartes seems to have thought that scientific knowledge is rather like the axioms and deductions of geometry. The problem is that scientific theories often derive from observation of some kind and are consequently more provisional. If someone claims that all frogs are amphibious, this relates to our existing knowledge of what frogs are and what amphibious behaviour is, but both concepts ultimately rely on our observations of frogs.

We can't work out certain truths about frogs just by using our minds.

Geometry and scientific facts are different things.

But Descartes thought that the world was essentially mathematical and could ultimately be studied and understood on that basis.

Logical and Causal Necessity

Descartes was also not wholly clear in his mind about the distinction between *causal* and *logical* necessity. If you say that 2+2 **must** be 4, then the "mustness" is logical. If your car breaks down and you say there **must** be a cause for it, the "mustness" is based on your past experiences with cars – the "mustness" is more psychological than logical. This confusion may have led Descartes into believing that you could have purely geometric and hence necessary knowledge of the physical world.

... the only principles we use are such as we see to be self-evident; if we infer nothing from them except by mathematical deduction and if all of these inferences agree accurately with natural phenomena; then we should, I think, be wronging God if we were to suspect this discovery of the causes to be delusive.

Can You Know Wax?

Descartes didn't think that observation was a complete waste of time. Investigating the world was useful – but only to confirm that your mathematical models were sound.

In one startling passage, Descartes claims that it is not really possible to know what "wax" is through the senses alone. When you look at wax, sometimes it is solid and sometimes liquid.

"… it has not completely lost the taste of honey; it retains some of the smell of the flowers from which it was gathered, its colour, shape, size are manifest; it is hard, cold and easily handled, and it gives out a sound if you rap it with your knuckle …"

"... the wax is put by the fire. It loses the remains of its flavour, the fragrance evaporates, the colour changes, the shape is lost, the size increases, it becomes fluid and hot, it can hardly be handled, and it will no longer give out a sound if you rap it. Is the same wax then, still there? Of course it is ..."

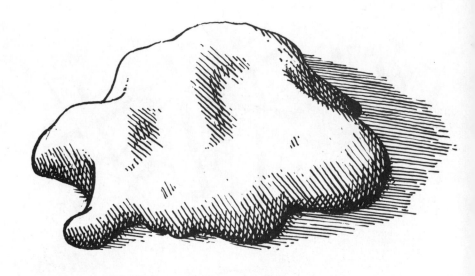

He then asks a rather odd question – how do we **know** that it is the same wax? It can't be through our senses which give us such contrary information about it. This means that *"I know the nature of this wax, not by imagination, but purely by mental perception ... I now know that even bodies are not perceived by the senses or the imaginative faculty but only by the intellect ..."*

It seems a rather odd thing to say. One reason for this view is that Descartes is a committed **Rationalist**.

Rationalists and Empiricists

Philosophers in the 17th and 18th centuries tend to get classified as either Rationalists or Empiricists. Rationalists think that the only reliable kind of knowledge has to come from our use of pure reason. They are usually enthusiastic about purely mental activities like mathematics and logic, and scathing about knowledge we get from our unreliable sense organs. For them there is no such thing as knowledge which belongs to the senses rather than to the mind.

This is why I think we can be sure about the measurable "primary qualities" of wax, but not its "secondary qualities" that we can only ever know through our senses.

FACULTY OF WAX STUDIES

Rationalists will always have difficulty in making room for any knowledge claims made about how the world really is, as opposed to the necessary but more remote claims derived from mathematics and logic.

Empiricist philosophers disagree. They believe that we can only really know what the external world is like by using our senses. We only know what wax is by seeing it, not by thinking about it. After we have used our senses, then we can form concepts of what kinds of objects we've been looking at.

And if we didn't actively apply these mental concepts to order and classify sensory information, we'd soon find the world an impossibly complex place to live in.

Nowadays the interminable debates between Rationalists and Empiricists seem rather pointless and sterile and Descartes' claim that only one kind of mental activity is valuable seems too dogmatic. It seems more sensible to say that our perception and reasoning actually work in tandem to form a composite interactive process that then generates knowledge.

But his theories on wax aren't what make Descartes an important philosopher. He is more popularly known as the man who began by saying that it was impossible to know *anything* at all – and that's what we have to look at next.

Brief History of Scepticism

Ever since human beings got themselves civilized and started asking questions, there have been irritating individuals called "Sceptics" who believe that human beings can never really know anything for sure. **Heraclitus** (c. 500 B.C.) thought that the world was totally unknowable because it was always changing.

That is why you can never step into the same river twice.

Cratylus (c. 400 B.C.) was even more radical.

No, you can't even step into the same river once! Both it and you are so changeable that words like "same" and "you" have no real meaning.

Cratylus was very suspicious of words. He thought that their meanings changed in the time it took for them to leave his mouth and enter other people's ears. So instead of talking, he just wagged his finger.

The Pyrrhonists

The first great Sceptics were called "Pyrrhonists", after **Pyrrho of Elis** (c. 360-272 B.C.). They were Athenians who taught at Plato's Academy in the 3rd and 4th centuries B.C. The later Roman thinker **Sextus Empiricus** (c. 200 A.D.) was their most famous spokesman because he produced a definitive textbook of their ideas and arguments. The Pyrrhonist big idea is a moral one.

> It is best not to go on a great quest for the truth because it will only make you miserable.

Sextus explains the two main Pyrrhonist arguments which show why real knowledge is always impossible.

The Pyrrhonist Arguments

All appearances are deceptive and therefore relative. This means that people's views about knowledge will always conflict. Different animals see the world in different ways, and there's no reason to believe that our singular human way of seeing the world is the "correct" one. Furthermore, human beings see the world differently depending on who and where they are.

A man standing on a cliff looking at a boat on the horizon will see the boat as small.

Whereas a man standing on the deck will believe it to be large.

So is the boat small or large? How can we ever really know who is right? All that we can really know is that we are ignorant.

The other argument is more difficult. If we are ever to accept something as **knowledge** then we have to find a proof or guarantee for it. This proof itself needs some kind of guarantee and so on, for ever and ever.

This impossibly endless chain of warranties means that human beings can never possess guaranteed or certain knowledge.

One obvious problem for the sceptics is that, if there is no such thing as knowledge, how can they themselves claim to know that all knowledge is an illusion? And the Pyrrhonist who said that he was happier without beliefs is fooling himself. Imagine this sceptic standing on the edge of a cliff, still waving at the small boat on the horizon. If he had no beliefs at all about body weight, gravity and dangerous places and fell off, he wouldn't be happy for long.

Sextus and Other Sceptics

Sextus Empiricus was also a doctor and would have been impressed by modern medical science. He was a pragmatic and rather unorthodox sceptic. He thought doctors should be guided by first impressions and past experience.

They can then make sensible empirical judgements about treatment, rather than trying to search for knowledge of mysterious and hidden causes of illness.

Pyrrhonists, however, never doubted that the physical world actually existed.

Human knowledge is very limited. Only divine revelation from God can reveal the truth to humble mortals.

The medieval Church father **St Augustine** (354-430)

Human beings have to be humble and aware of the severe limitations on what they can know for certain.

The early Renaissance scholar **Erasmus** (1466-1536)

I assembled a huge variety of different sceptical arguments in my **Apology for Raymond Sebond**.

Michel de Montaigne (1533-92)

But Descartes was more radical than any of them. In his **Meditations** (1641), he uses doubt much more aggressively and questions everything ruthlessly – even the certainties of mathematics, as well as the existence of the physical world.

And yet, paradoxically, I ended up by maintaining that there was one special thing it was impossible to be sceptical about – something that human beings could always know with absolute certainty.

Descartes began work on **Meditations** in 1639. He had been living a relatively solitary life in Holland for about ten years and this is the book that finally made his reputation as the most influential philosopher of the 17th century. The book is a vivid diary of his thoughts in the form of six Meditations, each one supposedly lasting a day.

Cartesian Doubt

Descartes' brand of scepticism is so unique that it is usually called "Cartesian Doubt". It is also systematic and more like a "method" than a declaration of religious piety.

In a letter he wrote to a friend, Descartes explained his special method of doubting like this …

Imagine someone has some apples which he wishes to store in a basket. A wise man will make quite sure that all the apples are perfect – because if an apple does go rotten then it will eventually infect all the others. So, any apple that has even the slightest blemish has to be ruthlessly rejected as unsuitable. This is exactly how Cartesian doubt works.

> You examine all human knowledge and see if it can be doubted. If it is **dubitable** and so "infected", then it must be mercilessly rejected as flawed.

Any "apple" of knowledge that is finally left behind after this procedure would obviously be very special. It would be the real thing – guaranteed, **indubitable** knowledge.

How to Doubt Everything

Descartes realized almost immediately that systematically doubting every single bit of human knowledge was impossible. He would have to repeat all the scientific experiments that had ever been performed, do all the mathematical deductions that had ever been calculated, visit all the regions of the world, read all the books ever written, and so on.

To get around this problem, I asked myself where all human knowledge comes from. I decided there are only two sources of knowledge: our senses and our reason.

Our knowledge of the material world comes through our five senses, whereas our knowledge of things like mathematics or logic comes through our reason. So, Descartes took a short cut by asking if these fundamental sources could themselves be doubted.

Seeing Isn't Believing

Descartes maintains that our human sense organs are often unreliable as sources of true knowledge. Although he never doubts that we do have sensory experiences, we have no way of knowing for sure what causes them. For example, you might be out walking on the moors and, through the mist, you see a man in the distance.

You call out to him but get no response. The man seems remarkably silent and immobile.

You get closer to him and find out that you had a long-distance conversation with a stone pillar!

Your senses have lied to you.

The problem is that you have no reliable way of knowing which of your two senses is the "correct" one. Descartes is not suggesting that our senses are always utterly unreliable. Presumably our sensory information gives us a rough approximation to what is "out there" – otherwise we wouldn't have survived for very long as a species. But the information that comes to us through our senses can be questioned and so must be ejected from the apple basket. A wise man no longer trusts that which has once deceived him. Knowledge produced by the senses is dubitable.

Dreaming

Most of us don't spend much of our time in deserts looking at mirages or being made dizzy by optical illusions. If you hold a pen in your hand and look at it in broad daylight in "optimum conditions", then surely you can be certain that the information given you by your senses is correct and reliable? How can you doubt that you are holding a pen and not something else? Descartes' second argument against the testimony of the senses is usually called the "Dreams argument".

It's quite simple: you might be dreaming that you are holding a pen. The actual truth is that you are asleep in bed and you are having an odd kind of pen-holding dream

mightier than the sword

It may not seem very likely to you that this is the case, but can you prove that it isn't? Descartes thought that you couldn't. There is no one obvious test that clearly and indubitably indicates which kind of mental state you are experiencing at any one time. You just can't **prove** that you aren't dreaming. Even close-up confrontational experiences can be doubted and so must be ejected from the basket.

Rationalists and Reason

We know that Descartes was a Rationalist philosopher who believed that reliable knowledge must come from reason, and not through our susceptible human senses. So his attacks on the reliability of the senses shouldn't come as a big surprise. **Plato** (c. 428-347 B.C.) had similar ideas two thousand years earlier. He agreed that only knowledge produced by rational minds could be reliable and stable.

> But I thought that we could always be certain about mathematics, geometry and logic. Such knowledge is pure and "necessary".

Two and two must and will always make four. So perhaps this kind of mental knowledge is unquestionable and so immune from highly corrosive Cartesian doubt?

The Invisible Demon

Descartes disagreed. Even mathematics and logic can be doubted in the end. He reminds us that we all commonly make mistakes in mathematics. So how do we know that we don't make errors all of the time?

We may **think** that mathematics is self-regulating and testable, but there might just be an **invisible demon** who continuously hypnotizes us into thinking that our mathematics is correct.

So, Descartes suggests, throughout history, human beings might have been doing maths wrongly. The invention of this special and rather odd invisible demon might seem like a desperate last-minute sceptical contrivance by Descartes. But his point is that even this "pure" knowledge, obtained through reason, is dubitable.

No sober person would accept that such an odd demon could exist, but none of us can prove that he doesn't.

Modern versions of the invisible demon argument involve horror stories of brains in jars being stimulated by electrodes or people strapped permanently into V.R. machines. If your senses were constantly being electrically stimulated to produce a whole series of ersatz "experiences" in your mind, or making you believe in odd mathematics – how would you ever know?

Do Our Senses Lie to Us?

Descartes' arguments seem very convincing. But they aren't always entirely plausible. We only know that our senses "lie" to us because, eventually, they then reveal the "truth". We ultimately know we've been talking to a stone pillar and not a man, because our eyes tell us so. But this doesn't invalidate Descartes' argument.

We still get conflicting messages from our senses and the information they produce, so they can be doubted.

Nevertheless, it's an odder argument than he admits. You could say that it's not our senses that lie to us, but our *interpretation* of the information they give us. Sensory information is mediated by us. We see a tall grey shape in the mist and we then infer that it's a man. Our sense of sight doesn't lie to us, it's we who misinterpret.

Are We Awake or Not?

And is it true to say that it's impossible to distinguish between our waking and dream experiences? It's possible that Descartes was quite sincere about this argument. His own dreams were often very vivid and he took them very seriously. But many people would say that our dream experiences are clearly distinguishable from conscious ones.

Dreams are illogical, they transcend time and space, break the normal laws of physics, are more involuntary, and so on.

There may not be **one** obvious test for dreams, but there probably is an alternative checklist of very good indicators.

Some philosophers also say that it just isn't possible to doubt whether you are sound asleep when you are, in fact, sound asleep, so there is something incoherent about Descartes' argument. Other philosophers and psychologists disagree – they think you can doubt in your dreams.

But I would respond by pointing out that we can never be absolutely and totally sure that we are awake. There is a smudge of doubt there that just cannot be erased.

Invisible Demons?

So, what about the "invisible demon"? Here Descartes does seem
to be desperate for a sceptical argument. Perhaps we are always
hallucinating and our senses are in thrall to a malicious (and extremely
busy) invisible demon. But can we seriously believe that "our"
mathematics is systematically wrong? If 2+2 "really" equals 5 or 3
and not 4, how can it be maths at all? This argument against rational
knowledge seems less convincing.

The Impossibility of a "Private Language"

There is also something very odd about this Cartesian kind of **universal scepticism**. Descartes always assumes that his thoughts are totally private and independent of the world.

But what is he thinking *with*? His thoughts are composed of words in either French or Latin. These words are part of a language which has a set of grammatical rules, conventional meanings, and a whole complex history and a culture behind it. None of that linguistic and cultural history can be doubted.

Having private sceptical thoughts in a private sceptical head is more difficult than it looks. Descartes also assumes that he is aware of his mental states of "knowing", "doubting", "being sure", and so on. So any philosopher who claims to be a total sceptic is really a bit of a fraud. Descartes came clean fairly early on.

I was dealing merely with the kind of extreme doubt which is metaphysical and exaggerated.

He always admitted he was playing a special kind of philosophical game – merely the temporary suspension of his beliefs. So by suspending some of them, he is actually holding other more sophisticated beliefs about why his temporary scepticism is necessary.

Back to the Basket

But, for a brief moment, Descartes almost convinces us that the apple basket of knowledge must remain empty. All of our knowledge might be contaminated at source. It may not be, but we cannot guarantee that it isn't. All of it can be doubted. Our senses might be lying to us, we could be dreaming, or an invisible demon might be fooling us. It's the cumulative effect of all of these arguments that is ultimately so powerful and convincing.

We can't even guarantee that we have bodies, only that we have minds.

And if Descartes was a true sceptic, his philosophy would have ended there and he could have gone back to growing vegetables in his garden. But he isn't a true sceptic. There is one extraordinary apple left that has the right to remain in the basket.

The Last Apple: Cogito ergo Sum

By going through this process of rigorous doubt, Descartes eventually discovered something rather extraordinary. What he realized was that there was always one thing that he could never doubt – the fact that he was doubting or thinking. And thinking just can't happen in mid-air. There has to be a consciousness or mind doing it, so Descartes can't doubt that he exists either. Hence the famous **Cogito ergo Sum** – "I think therefore I am". Or perhaps more accurately: there are thoughts, so there must be a mind.

While I could pretend that I had no body and that there was no world ... I could not, for all that, pretend that I did not exist. I saw this from the mere fact that I thought of doubting the truth of other things.

So, wonderfully and paradoxically, as soon as you try to doubt the Cogito, you confirm it. It is a truth that has no dependency on the senses, and even more remarkably, is also immune from the attentions of the invisible demon.

We could, for instance, be hypnotized by the demon into thinking that we have legs and were walking, but we just can't be fooled about doubting. At last Descartes has a perfect indubitable apple to put in the basket.

What is the Cogito?

The Cogito is an extraordinary discovery and the first principle of all of Descartes' work. It has influenced all kinds of modern philosophy, as well as literature, art, social science and religion. **Jean-Paul Sartre** (1905-80) founded his version of Existentialist philosophy on it. The issues and problems that it raises have kept many philosophers in work for many years. It is still not wholly clear exactly what the "Cogito" actually is.

It's certainly not as "clear and distinct" as Descartes thought it was.

Because it's not clear that we are directly aware of ourselves in the way he says we are.

Some philosophers believe the Cogito is a real factual discovery about human beings and the universe (a "synthetic" proposition).

Others say it is merely a statement which clarifies the meaning and interrelatedness of concepts like "thought" and "existence" (merely an empty "analytic" proposition).

It remains one of the most important discoveries of Western philosophy and perhaps marks the spot where modern philosophy begins and Scholasticism ends. It also began a branch of philosophy now called the Philosophy of Mind – about which there is more later in this book.

The Cul de Sac of the Cogito

But wonderfully certain though the Cogito is, it seems to be a bit of a dead end. If you doubt or think, then, at that exact moment, you can guarantee that your mind exists or that you are conscious. But this kind of temporary private knowledge is of limited use.

I was always clear in my own mind that my radical system of doubt was just a beginning.

The Cogito is a unique discovery, but not the ultimate destination of Descartes' philosophical efforts. He was more ambitious – he wanted to be certain of more than just his own private subjective consciousness. He wanted to reinvent the foundations and structure of *all* human knowledge.

Public Knowledge

Knowledge has to be **public** so that it can be read about in books and journals and kept in libraries. It is vital that scientific knowledge is repeatable, testable and democratic, otherwise it remains no more than personal beliefs in the privacy of an individual mind. Descartes compares the limited certainty of the Cogito to an *"acrobat who always lands on his feet"*.

Progress is always slow and limited. How are we always to find truths such as we can be as firmly convinced of them as we are of our own existence?

The Clear and Distinct Rule

So Descartes had to convert the private temporary knowledge of the Cogito into something which is more public and permanent. He felt that if he could discover what it is about the Cogito that makes it so certain, then he should be able to uncover a universal rule which would offer similar guarantees of certainty about other kinds of knowledge. He tried to produce this rule with an argument like this:

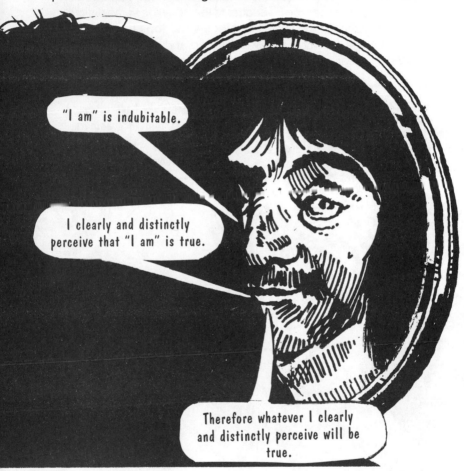

"I am" is indubitable.

I clearly and distinctly perceive that "I am" is true.

Therefore whatever I clearly and distinctly perceive will be true.

The "clear and distinct" rule is the first one from the **Discourse on the Method**, where it is a statement of caution. Now, in the **Meditations**, it becomes a powerful tool of discovery which Descartes believes will enable him to jump from this limited, private certainty to a broader, more flexible certainty about other kinds of knowledge.

Problems of the Clear and Distinct Rule

Descartes shared the view of many 17th century philosophers that thinking about ideas in our minds is rather like watching a kind of mental cinema screen. An idea should hit us with the same clarity and immediacy as objects hit our eyes when we see them. But Descartes' explanation of the "clear and distinct" rule isn't itself very clear. He seems to change his mind both about what it is and about how important or reliable it is. In the **Discourse** he suggests that "there is some difficulty about what is distinct", and yet in the later **Meditations** he maintains that "we cannot be in error in this way". "Clear" and "distinct" are relative terms. What is clear and distinct to you may be very fuzzy to me.

If someone does have a clear and distinct idea of a unicorn, it's not exactly a guarantee of any truth about its existence.

There's nothing to stop the invisible demon from inserting ideas of breathtaking clarity into our minds in order to fool us.

This is why Descartes has to bring God into it.

The Need for God

Before Descartes can rely on the "clear and distinct rule", he needs to remove the threat of the evil demon. The best way to do this is to bring in a God who will never deceive us and will always guarantee that any clear and distinct ideas that enter our minds will be true. So Descartes has to set out to prove that God exists. He begins by saying that he already has a clear and distinct idea of God in his mind. His ideas about God are the standard and traditional theological ones about a perfect, infinite, immutable and permanent being.

The Trademark Argument

Descartes' argument is often known as the "Trademark" argument. When a manufacturer makes a product, he usually stamps his logo onto it.

When God makes us, He stamps the innate idea of Himself into our minds.

Descartes thought that human beings were all born with a rather odd mix of innate ideas, including those of mathematics, the soul and God's existence. He then relies on the old and odd Scholastic "Causal Adequacy Principle" to reinforce his claim. The Principle relies on a set of beliefs.

God may well exist, but not because of the Causal Adequacy Principle. Ideas in the mind are "real" in a very different sort of way from the way in which things or beings are "real" – even divine ones. It seems that some of the old Scholastic doctrines were still very difficult for Descartes to discard. He was a great and original thinker, but, like all of us, also a product of his time.

The Cartesian Circle

But what is worse, Descartes' argument is now infamous for being the "Cartesian circle". Descartes uses that which he wishes to prove as one of his premises. You can't guarantee the clear and distinct rule with a truth-telling Deity if you've already claimed that you know he exists because you have a clear and distinct idea of him in your mind. Descartes needs God to guarantee his rule and the rule to guarantee that God exists.

The Ontological Argument

Descartes also produced his own variation of yet another old Scholastic argument for the existence of God, known as the "Ontological" argument. The theologian **St Anselm** (1033-1109) is usually given the credit for inventing it. The argument goes like this.

1. God is a totally perfect being.

2. Total perfection must involve existence.

Because ideas are inferior to things that exist – remember? And if God is perfect, he can't be a mere inferior **idea**, can he?

3. Therefore God exists.

ANSELM

Descartes' Ontological argument is slightly different. His clear and distinct idea of God is of a totally perfect being, so God must be totally perfect, and so on.

A Series of Leaky Proofs

The Ontological proof for God's existence isn't very convincing. You attempt to magic God into existence through the way you define him, as if words had the power to make ideas real.

Descartes wants us to accept that our knowledge of the external world is flawed or even hallucinatory. Yet, at the same time, he wants us to accept that all clear and distinct ideas are true and that they will be guaranteed by a Deity whose existence he then tries to prove with a series of leaky "proofs". What Descartes is up against is the fundamental problem for all Rationalist philosophers.

If knowledge has to be appropriated by the mind and not the senses, what kind of guarantee can we have that we are not thinking absolute nonsense?

FUNCTION ROOM
★ TUESDAY: 7:30
RATIONALISTS CLUB
MEMBERS ONLY
NO GUESSING
★ THURSDAY: 8:00
LINE DANCING.

Descartes' "solution" is that God has created eternal truths about us and the world and that, if we perceive them as clear and distinct, then they are guaranteed.

Making Mistakes

Another worry for Descartes is that, if God guarantees clear and distinct ideas, why is it that conscientious people still make mistakes? Much depends on how you view human potential. Some philosophers, like **Benedictus de Spinoza** (1632-77), believe that human ability is virtually infinite in capacity.

Given enough time, the human mind could mature and grow until it became virtually infallible and could see "the big picture".

I'm more pessimistic. For me, the human mind will always be finite and capable of error. Only God can have this kind of infinite mental capacity.

Intellect versus Will

Descartes has a theory about why the human mind will always be of limited ability.

We come to believe or make judgements about things after exercising two of our faculties – our intellect and our free will. Our minds may decide that the angles of a triangle add up to 180 degrees, but then we have to **choose** to believe that this is so. Provided we always choose clear and distinct ideas, then, according to Descartes, we cannot make mistakes.

The problem is that we often choose to believe confused, unclear ideas. Our will power is often more influential than our intellect.

Our freedom to choose is itself infinite and is a gift from God – to a large extent, it is what makes us human.

But it is the overriding power of this free will which is the reason why we often do fall disastrously into error. As human beings we tend to exercise our freedom of choice way beyond the confines of the clear and distinct ideas arrived at by the understanding. For some reason, God has given us total freedom but limited understanding.

The only remedy is for us to restrain our will and abstain from judgement more than we do, and to restrict our knowledge claims to clear and distinct ideas.

With this explanation, Descartes has been able to hold on to his doctrine of divinely certified clear and distinct ideas, and at the same time to explain why human beings get things wrong all the time.

Belief Is Cheap

Descartes does not altogether provide a plausible explanation of human error. It seems odd to suggest that we constantly believe things that we don't understand. If we don't understand quantum theory, how can we believe it? Descartes' answer is that "understanding" means "fully understanding". We may **think** we understand something, but we don't. Belief is cheap. True understanding is less frequent than we realize.

It's clear and distinct to most people that smoking causes lung cancer, but cigarettes still sell.

Belief and Faith

When we recognize that 2+2 = 4, then, according to Descartes, we perceive this mathematics as a clear and distinct idea, and then choose to believe it or make a "judgement" about it. But when we "perceive" that 2+2 = 4, it's not obvious whether we are holding an idea in our minds or making some kind of decision about that idea. If we hold clear and distinct ideas in our minds, then, in a way, we have already made a decision about their status. There is something odd about linking choosing and believing in the way Descartes does.

It's as if Descartes confuses belief with faith.

A Good Bet

This confusion between belief and faith is often a problem for Descartes. Belief is connected with rationality and evidence. Faith is not really a kind of belief, but more an act of will. If, for example, you think that God's existence is provable, then you don't need to have faith in Him. But the Church often insists that Christians need both belief and faith. The French thinker **Blaise Pascal** (1623-62) famously suggested that it is rational to choose to believe in God. This is known as "Pascal's wager".

Even if the evidence for God's existence is slim, a sensible gambler will choose to believe in Him, since to do so is a good bet.

If I'm wrong, well, death is final. If I'm right, then everlasting bliss awaits me.

But is this gamble an example of belief or faith?

By Section Four of **Meditations**, Descartes thinks he has fixed a rule for establishing truth, validated God's existence, proved the facts of his own consciousness and existence, explained why human beings make mistakes and suggested that God is the guarantor of certain rather special ideas in our minds. Descartes has reinstated the status of the sort of knowledge that we acquire through our reason and intellect.

A Quiet Life in Holland

When Descartes was writing his philosophy, he needed total peace and quiet. He also became increasingly tired of certain individuals attempting to embroil him in various kinds of religious controversy. For these good reasons, he didn't like too many people to know his address in Holland. He moved several times and had all his mail directed to the house of his friend Mersenne.

I have told Mersenne to lie to everyone about where I live.

RENÉ DOESN'T LIVE HERE ANY MORE.

One man who did manage to track him down was called de Sorbière. He spent much of his time going around Europe as a kind of amateur collector of intellectuals. He arrived unannounced at Descartes' retreat and was received with remarkable politeness. He described Descartes' life like this.

He was in a little château of fine situation about two hours from the sea. He had a sufficient staff of servants ... a nice garden with an orchard beyond it; and all around pastures from which stood out steeples of various heights, till in the far horizon they seemed mere points. He could go in a day by canal to Utrecht, Rotterdam, Haarlem or Amsterdam.

DING-DONG!

In middle age, Descartes started wearing wigs made specially in Paris. He had a collection of four when he died. He was a neat dresser and usually wore black. He carried a sword when he travelled any distance from home. He lived a very simple life for a gentleman.

A diet of roots and fruits prolongs life, so I eat meat very rarely.

His favourite dish was omelette made from eggs that he always insisted were at least ten days old.

Although he took exercise every day, he nevertheless spent at least twelve hours every day in bed, where he did most of his thinking and some of his writing.

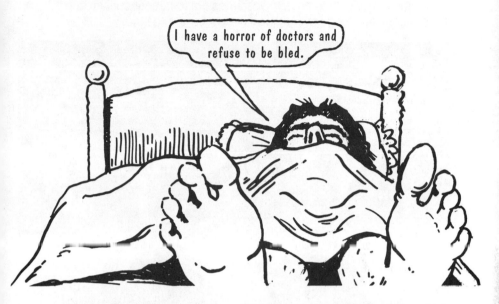

He regarded his own body as if it were a well-made machine which would work best if regularly exercised and left to its own devices.

Descartes had few servants. He was always very generous to them, and sometimes to strangers. One day an impoverished peasant shoemaker called Rembrantsz arrived at his large house in Endegeest and asked to see the famous philosopher. The servants sent him away twice without telling their master. Descartes got to hear about him and subsequently had long philosophical discussions with him.

Descartes was a compulsive letter writer. He wrote several every evening and one long letter every fortnight to his childhood friend Mersenne. He corresponded with the obscure and the famous in many different countries. He insisted that prose style should be simple, clear and direct at all times. He was in favour of more widespread literacy and thought the spelling of words should reflect the way they were pronounced.

At various times Descartes expressed an interest in a Universal Language.

It is probably best to adapt Latin to this end, rather than invent a new language from scratch.

He also thought it would be a good idea to invent a special philosophical language in which it would always be possible for men to think clearly.

Meditations on Perception

In Meditations 5 and 6, Descartes goes on to ask whether it is possible to restore the knowledge that we acquire through perception. He thinks that we can now be certain of mathematical ideas, but what kind of knowledge can we get of the external world outside of our minds? It's a problem for Descartes and all Rationalist philosophers.

You can have lots of clear and distinct ideas about triangles and triangularity, but can you ever know whether any actually exist in the world?

Clear and distinct ideas are "determinant" – they describe the "essences" of things but do not help us to know whether there's any chance of ever seeing them.

Descartes was quite happy to admit that we do have sensory experiences but maintained that we never have these experiences directly. He is a "representative realist" who believes that we only ever perceive the world indirectly through internal mental images or ideas.

LOFTY THOUGHT

We can be certain that we are experiencing **something** in our minds, but what is causing that something is uncertain.

But, if God is good, why would he equip us with senses that are so indirect and unreliable? What is Descartes' answer to this?

Bringing in God Again

Descartes' answer is a bit of a compromise, and relies on an appeal to God's goodness a second time. He is convinced that at least those clear and distinct ideas that enter our minds about material objects must reflect some form of external reality. If we have certain clear and distinct ideas of objects in the world, then God will guarantee that these ideas will correspond to what is actually "out there". But the only clear and distinct ideas we can be sure of are mathematical ideas.

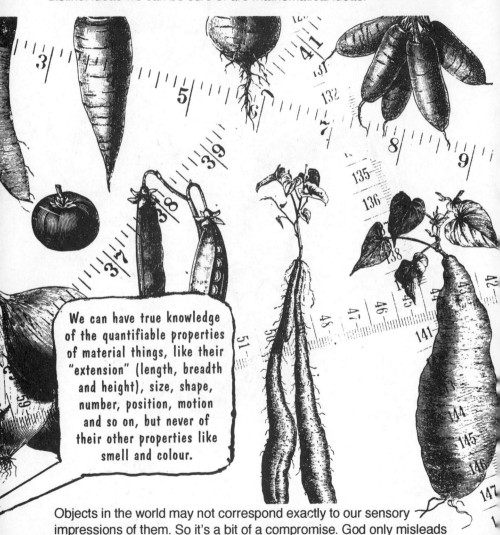

We can have true knowledge of the quantifiable properties of material things, like their "extension" (length, breadth and height), size, shape, number, position, motion and so on, but never of their other properties like smell and colour.

Objects in the world may not correspond exactly to our sensory impressions of them. So it's a bit of a compromise. God only misleads us some of the time.

Mathematical Certainties

This is the point Descartes is making when he examines the piece of wax. When cold, it appears to be hard and even audible. When hot, it becomes liquid and silent. Because it is a "body", he can be certain that it is "extended" – even though it is a very protean three-dimensional object.

Its true mathematical nature can always be perceived by the mind alone.

This seems an odd belief – that we know what wax is purely from an exercise of the mind, independent of our senses. His point may be a good scientific one, though. It is the underlying mathematical structure of things that gives us the real truth about them. The belief that true knowledge has to be mathematical – of that which is stable and unchanging – is not new to Descartes, as we'll see next.

Ancient Greek Mathematics

The ancient Greeks were the first to recognize that numbers seemed to have an odd life of their own. **Pythagoras** (c. 550-500 B.C.) was so impressed by them that he thought they should be worshipped!

The visible world is merely an illusion that hides the real mathematical reality of things.

$a^2 + b^2 = c^2$

Mathematics exists separately from human beings and is prior to the creation of the universe itself.

There are "Platonist" mathematicians who tend to agree with the view of Plato that mathematics "pre-exists" and is the real structure of the universe.

Is the Universe Mathematical?

The way that the number Pi keeps cropping up as a constant in all sorts of practical mathematical problems seems to indicate that maths is embedded in the material world in some way.

Sunflowers and pine cones follow Fibonacci numbers (1, 2, 3, 5, 8, 13, 21, 34 etc.).

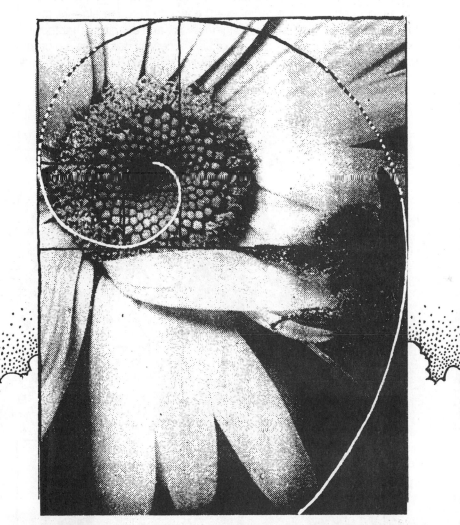

And even apparently random and chaotic things like clouds follow fractal geometric patterns. Maths seems to be universal.

Descartes the Mathematician

Descartes is famous as a mathematician as well as a philosopher. He gave his name to "Cartesian coordinates" and began certain conventions now common to mathematicians, like representing unknowns by the letters x, y and z and knowns by a, b, and c. He invented the modern way of expressing squares and cubes by using small numbers (as in 4^2). He greatly advanced analytic geometry, which generally makes solving geometric problems simpler. In **La Géométrie**, Descartes showed how you can use algebra to recognize many typical problems in geometry and bring together those which are related. Partly because of his success in doing this, he came to believe that all human knowledge could eventually be mathematized.

The Rigour of Mathematics

In the last of his three famous dreams, Descartes believed he had been shown the way in which to unite the whole of science with this one "method" of mathematics. Mathematics, and especially geometry, offer guarantees and a deductive rigour that made a deep impression on Descartes. If you accept a few "self-evident" axioms in geometry like "parallel lines never meet" and "the shortest distance between two points is a straight line", then it is possible from such small beginnings to deduce a rich body of reliable knowledge. Descartes obviously thought that similarly large amounts of knowledge were obtainable from his axiom that "matter is extended substance".

But What is Mathematics?

So mathematics does seem universal. That's why, if we want to contact beings in other galaxies, it makes sense to broadcast mathematical and not linguistic messages.

No one quite knows what mathematics actually is, and some mathematicians aren't very sure themselves. It's still not clear whether mathematics is something we *invent* or something we have *discovered*.

Mathematical Relativism

The reassuring view of a single universal mathematics has been challenged by the more recent invention (or discovery!) of very plausible and successful "alternative geometries". Before this happened, everyone thought that **Euclid** (c. 300 B.C.) had "discovered" the one true geometry encoded in the universe. It now seems reasonable to suppose that there is nothing ubiquitous about Euclidean geometry. It may be a localized human investigative tool that just happens to make good sense to us.

Formalists

This relativist or "Formalist" view states that mathematics is no more than a human invention, a closed and "empty" system of deductions produced from a set of initial self-evident axioms. Formalists declare that mathematics does not reveal the mysteries of the universe to us, but is really more like chess – a self-regulating and consistent game.

This means that mathematics can produce elegant and complex "models" of truth, but cannot ever be the truth itself.

Because mathematics is a "closed" system, it is hard to see how it could provide us with "new" knowledge about anything other than itself. Maths for the formalists can only ever be valid or invalid. Words like "true" or "false" just don't apply.

The Success Story

Descartes himself was a committed Platonist. He thought that reason would discover scientific truth – and his confidence is based on a faith in mathematics. He seems to have believed that all human problems could eventually be mathematized. To some extent this vision of his has become a reality.

In our own day, theoretical sciences like nuclear physics, astrophysics, chemistry, genetics, ecology, economics, linguistics and computer sciences would not exist without mathematics.

In the last years of the 20th century, scientists hope and believe that they will discover the last great unifying theory of all – the Theory of Everything (or T.O.E.) – uniting the laws of gravity, electromagnetism, radioactivity and the strong nuclear force (that holds neutrons and protons together inside the nucleus).

Mathematical Humans

Many mathematicians are still resolute Cartesians. As mathematical human beings, we believe that the universe is mathematically organized and patterned, and, so far, for us, it seems to be that way. When we investigate very small nuclear particles or very remote black holes, mathematics seems to describe and explain such strange phenomena with clarity and predictive power.

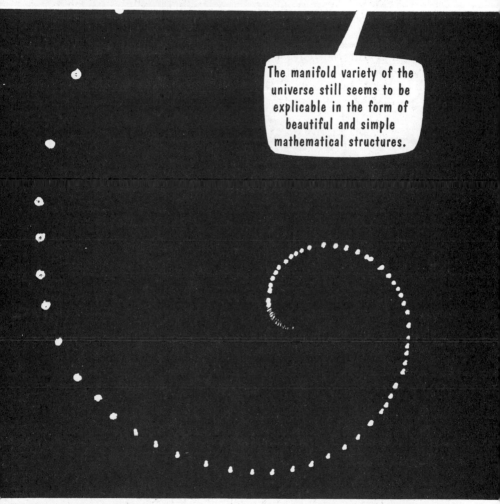

The manifold variety of the universe still seems to be explicable in the form of beautiful and simple mathematical structures.

Even more surprisingly, scientists continually find that previously invented "Formalist" mathematics subsequently often has practical "Platonist" applications.

The Mathematization of Everything

No one really knows for sure whether "our" mathematics provides us with useful models that offer us only approximate guides to what the universe is like, or whether it tells us the whole truth and nothing but. Descartes' dream has made modern science possible and powerful in ways that he could never have imagined.

Most modern scientists would probably also stress how much science still has to be empirical.

A blind faith in the power of mathematical deductive models certainly led Descartes to some very odd conclusions in the natural sciences.

Mathematical reasoning reveals that water freezes more rapidly when it is boiled.

This presumably can only be established by conducting an experiment.

Mathematicians don't have a way of establishing such empirical truths, however elegant their maths might be.

Mathematics has some small part to play in the human sciences, such as psychology and sociology, but, so far, human emotions, behaviour, culture, history and civilization itself seem safe from the grasp of mathematical formulae. (Although some philosophers and mathematicians believe that one day there may be newer and more flexible kinds of "soft maths" that may succeed in doing this.)

Res Extensa

Descartes held to the Pythagorean and Platonist ideas that the visible world is merely an illusion that hides the mathematical reality of things.

So there is nothing especially new about Descartes' view that we can only ever have knowledge of the mathematically certain *res extensa* (the width, breadth and height of matter that occupies space).

> Such knowledge is safe and secure because it lies in the geometric world of clear and distinct propositions.

Properties like hardness and colour are relative, unmeasurable, and are subjective sensations produced in human minds by the objects, but not actually present in them. So objects possess reliable "primary qualities" as well as the odder and more puzzling "secondary qualities".

For Descartes, the universe is already encoded with mathematical information which it is the job of mathematicians to detect.

Mathematical knowledge is the only kind we can ever have about the world which is **true**.

This mathematical vision encouraged Descartes to depict the universe as one huge singular thing which occupies space. His cerebral and abstract picture of the world is a grey and prosaic one – as if everything in the universe is reduced to a universal homogenous grey "extended" porridge.

So, for Descartes, virtually everything that exists is *res extensa* – matter which can be mathematically measured and known for certain by the human mind. Descartes' view of the human body follows on from this.

It is just a kind of sophisticated machine which can be reduced to the same physical basis as everything else in the world.

He thought that this was obviously the case with all our non-conscious physical functions like breathing and blinking. This opinion led Descartes to his extraordinary and chilling belief that animals were non-conscious and so the noises they made when being vivisected were only those a machine would make when being disassembled. Screams of pain were just mechanical noises!

This was the rather gruesome side to Descartes' intellectual activities. He viewed all animal and human bodies as mere animated machines, and so enjoyed disassembling them to see how they "worked". He must have startled some of the butchers in Amsterdam. He daily visited their shops and took home rather large parts of various animals which he then dissected.

I also vivisected some rabbits, fish and eels for the purpose of watching the operations of the heart and the movement of the blood in the arteries.

He also owned a pet dog called "Monsieur Grat", which he fortunately left intact.

Because of his interest in automata, Descartes once had one made in the likeness of a young girl which could make some human-like noises and move its limbs. He took the ingenious device on board a ship, packed in a box. Unfortunately the ship's captain was curious about the box, thinking perhaps that Descartes was a kidnapper.

He threw it overboard, convinced that the horrible thing had to be the work of the devil. Descartes was not pleased. *SO THE STORY GOES....*

Res Cogitans

The one thing that doesn't fit into Descartes' materialist picture is the human being or *res cogitans* – the "thinking substance". Descartes still employed terms like "substance" and "essence" from Scholastic philosophy. A "substance" is something that is unique and depends on nothing else for its existence. The "essence" of something is that element of it which makes it part of a class.

It can have other "accidental" properties like its size, but that's not the "essential" property that makes it a triangle. So it is the "essence" of a mind that it thinks.

Cartesian Dualism

Descartes came up with the idea that human beings are made of **two** substances. They have conscious minds as well as physical bodies. So there are two kinds of substance in the world – minds and matter.

This "Cartesian dualism" is fundamental to all of Descartes' philosophy. It sounds very familiar to everyone in the Western world because of the Christian doctrine which declares that all human beings have "souls". Descartes remained a Catholic all his life and thought that he could give the doctrine of souls philosophical respectability. And even people with no strong religious beliefs are still rather fond of this psychological and emotional "picture" of what constitutes human beings. Many of us would like to think that our minds are not mortal.

The Dualist Argument

Descartes' view of the soul isn't exactly orthodox Christianity. He uses words like "mind", "soul" and "intellect" interchangeably, and they all refer to the same thing, even if they have rather different connotations. (The word "soul" didn't always signify some immortal entity for thinkers in the 17th century, although Descartes himself did see it that way.) In the second Meditation, he attempts to prove the proposition that minds or souls are totally different from bodies. (The word "body" for Descartes means any physical object that occupies space, so the human body is a "body"!) His argument goes something like this.

THAT I **EXIST** IS INDUBITABLE (CAN'T BE DOUBTED)

THAT I HAVE A **BODY** IS DUBITABLE (CAN BE DOUBTED)

SO, MY **EXISTENCE** IS INDEPENDENT OF MY **BODY**.

SO, I CAN'T BE CERTAIN THAT I **EXIST** WHEN I'M NOT **THINKING**.

SO, MY EXISTENCE **DEPENDS** ON MY **THINKING**.

THEREFORE, I AM, IN ESSENCE, A **THINKING THING** OR A **SOUL**, **MIND**, AN **INTELLECT**.

Thinking Existence

What defines human beings is that they *think*, not that they have a
physical existence.

From this I knew I was a substance whose whole essence or nature is simply to think, and which does not require any place, or depend on any material thing in order to exist. ... Accordingly this "I" is entirely distinct from the body.

It's a complex argument, with rather startling conclusions. One is that our existence depends entirely on our being *conscious*. Once we stop thinking, then we disappear!

If mind is to exist, then to do so it has to think continually — even in sleep and early childhood.

Another conclusion is that our minds or souls continue to exist when our bodies die.

So Descartes' dualism adds weight to the traditional Christian idea that our true selves exist somehow independently of our physical bodies.

Problems with Cartesian Dualism

It's very reassuring, but not very logical. Just because we are unable to doubt that we are thinking but **can** doubt that we have bodies doesn't **prove** that we exist separately from our bodies. Descartes implies that if something can be doubted, then we should proceed on the assumption that it is false rather than uncertain.

So — if we cannot guarantee that we have bodies, then we should assume that we don't — which is a very odd statement.

¼ POUNDER WITH CHEESE

It would be rather like saying that because I can doubt that there is life on other planets, then there isn't. He's using the act of doubting as a kind of proof.

Another Argument

Later on, in the sixth Meditation, Descartes employs another argument to prove that human beings consist of two kinds of substance. He uses his "clear and distinct rule" again.

Because I can clearly and distinctly perceive the mind as existing separately from the body, then the mind must have a separate existence of its own.

It's not a very impressive argument – again, partly because of the internal weaknesses and ambiguities of the "rule" itself.

Human Beings and Language

Descartes also thought that there was some empirical evidence for his dualist doctrine. Human beings signal their uniqueness by the ways in which they use language. Human beings aren't like programmed linguistic machines.

They respond verbally to different situations in a huge variety of often unpredictable ways. Animals aren't like this. They aren't conscious, and so their behaviour and language are repetitive and mechanical.

If you teach a magpie to say good-day to its mistress when it sees her approach ... it will be the expression of the hope of eating. ... But the use of words, so defined, is peculiar to human beings.

Nowadays we might say that human linguistic ingenuity and flexibility are "stimulus-free" and a direct result of how our brains are wired up thanks to our complex evolutionary history. But for Descartes, the immense flexibility of human linguistic responses was yet another proof of the existence of an immortal thinking soul.

Brains or Minds?

So, is he right? Are we immortal souls? For Descartes, consciousness and thinking are clear and immediate, as if our minds were always transparent and open to inspection. But it's not at all clear that thinking and consciousness are non-corporeal processes. Most philosophers and neuroscientists would now say that we all need physical brains for these events to take place.

It's true that we do have immediate access to the private thoughts going on in our heads.

But this doesn't mean that there aren't physical, chemical and electrical processes going on "behind" all the thinking and allowing it to happen in the first place.

That which actually does the thinking is probably a physical thing – the brain.

Effects of Brain Damage

Neuroscientists who conduct experiments with patients who have suffered from brain damage have no doubt at all that thinking minds are physiological phenomena.

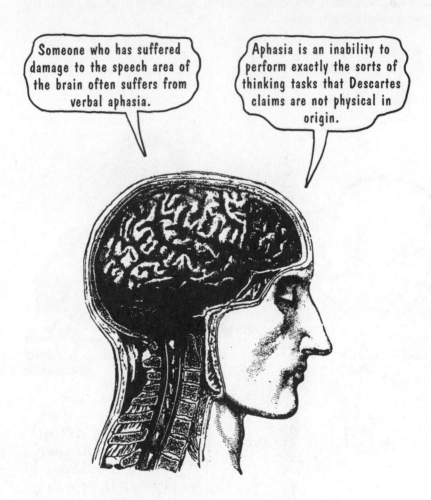

This means that damage to our brain will usually greatly impair our mental processes. If the body ceases to exist, then so will thought. Descartes disagreed. He maintained that the mind would continue to have abstract conceptual thoughts after the extinction of the physical body and the brain. It sounds a rather dull sort of afterlife.

Mind-Body Interaction

Another obvious problem for Cartesian dualism is mind-body interaction. If human beings consist of two utterly distinct substances, then they just can't interact. But it is fairly obvious that a mental event, like that of choosing, can cause a physical one to occur. (You want a piece of cake, so your arm reaches out for one). A physical event can also cause a mental one. (My body feels the pain of a pin stuck into my arm which then registers strongly in my mind.)

But if the mind is a wholly non-physical "soul", how can it cause the body to perform certain movements?

How can thoughts "push"? And how can physical events like pain experienced by the body affect the mind? And if mind is non-extended (does not exist in time or space in the way that bodies do), where does this interaction take place?

Descartes wisely gave up on this problem in the end, but initially he did attempt to explain how it is that soul-like minds and physical bodies can interact.

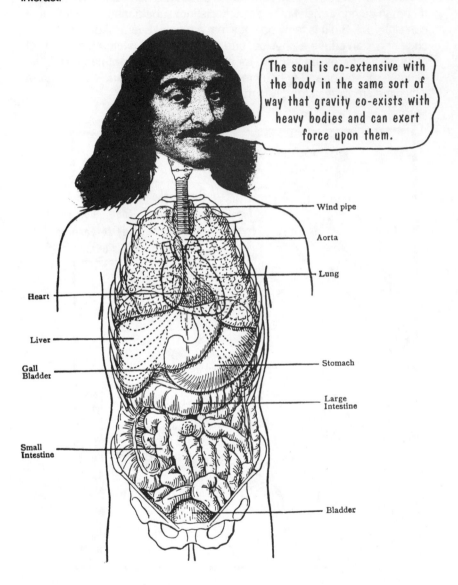

The soul is co-extensive with the body in the same sort of way that gravity co-exists with heavy bodies and can exert force upon them.

Wind pipe

Aorta

Lung

Heart

Liver

Gall Bladder

Stomach

Large Intestine

Small Intestine

Bladder

He thinks this explains why we feel the pain of a gash in the hand in a very immediate, powerful way. Human pain is not perceived in a remote intellectual way, like the way in which a ship's captain "perceives" a gash in his ship's hull.

But this co-extensive view must be incorrect if soul or mind are non-extended and do not exist in time or space. Descartes finally thought that there must be a part of the brain in which this interaction occurred.

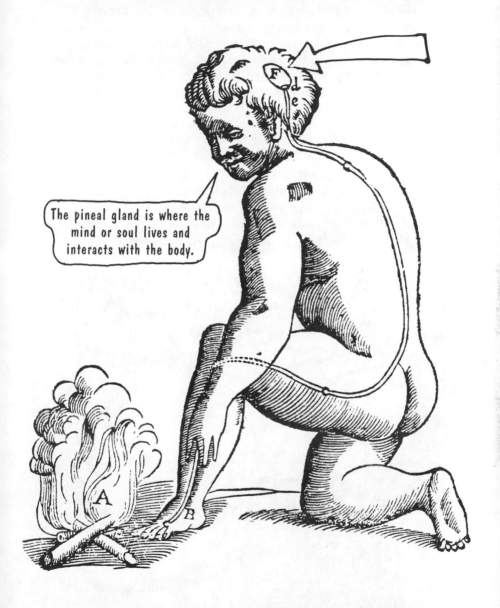

The pineal gland is where the mind or soul lives and interacts with the body.

But even if that were true – determining **where** spiritual and physical interaction takes place doesn't explain **how** it takes place.

Seeing and Hearing the World

Although Descartes was usually committed to his dualist view, he was prepared to qualify it in certain ways. The problem of mind-body interaction became even more obvious when he examined certain kinds of mental experiences, like seeing and hearing, which presumably depend on the existence of an external world. Descartes imagines the soul to be rather like a little person or "homunculus" experiencing the world by some kind of internal process like watching an internal cinema screen.

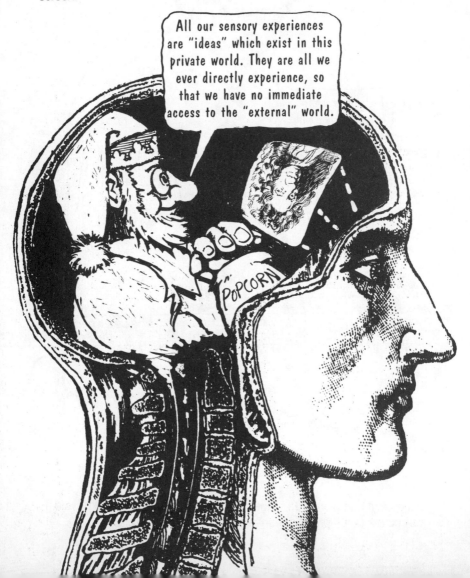

All our sensory experiences are "ideas" which exist in this private world. They are all we ever directly experience, so that we have no immediate access to the "external" world.

This is a confusing account of seeing and hearing. It seems odd to talk about perceiving the world as if it is a similar process to how we think about ideas. And more confusingly, ideas are often talked about by Descartes as if they were objects. This kind of talk about perception led English empiricist philosophers like **John Locke** (1632-1704) into an impossible linguistic and conceptual maze for many years.

Perceiving and Imagining

Descartes thought that sensory experiences were a composite of both mental and physical processes. Doubting and understanding are purely mental and non-physiological, but other mental processes like perceiving and imagining are a mixture of the two. Descartes thought that imagining depended on our previous experiences of the world.

Our imagination is slower and less adequate because it involves physical processes in the brain.

So, some mental states are body-dependent, but others, like doubting, are "purer" and would survive the death of the body.

Trialism Explains Sensations

Descartes' philosophy of mind isn't relentlessly and simplistically dualist. Some thought processes are purely mental, others are an odder kind of mental-physical hybrid. Descartes eventually held a rather tentative but more sophisticated kind of "trialist" view of the world and the people in it. If we look at a frog, then certain physical processes occur in our eyes, optical nerves and our brains. Our sensory experiences of the frog will tell us what colour it is and what noises it makes. Our minds will then make judgements about its shape, size, weight, and so on.

Human beings have bodies which are "extended" and subject to physical forces in the world like all matter. But they are **res cogitans** as well. They can doubt, make judgements and understand with their minds.

And they also experience sensations such as those of pain, hunger, sound and colour – sensations which have both physical and mental ingredients.

In the earlier dualist model, rocks, animals and human bodies are things which possess merely extension. Human beings also possess thought but their sensations remain unexplained. The trialist view seems to make more sense.

Rocks and all "bodies" remain as extensive things, but animals are now beings that have sensations. Human beings are extended bodies, experiencers of sensation and non-corporeal minds.

Although the trialist view has its own problems, it does seem to be a more flexible account of what human beings are actually like.

However, Descartes never really pursued this "trialist" view with any rigour. His main view of us is still the rather cold and abstract one of minds inhabiting bodies. As human beings, we are not like that. We are beings that feel, imagine and experience, as well as think and exist. Cartesian "people" still don't seem like fully qualified human beings to most of us.

The Philosophy of Mind

Descartes' conclusions are strange. But almost single-handedly, he began a whole branch of philosophy now known as the **Philosophy of Mind**. Minds are still a puzzle. We all have them, although there is some doubt about how long for. If we think about minds as if they are physical objects in the world, then **how** they exist is very problematic. Minds clearly do exist, but not in the same way that arms and legs exist. For Descartes, minds exist as souls – in a non-extended, non-physical way. For materialists, this kind of explanation of minds is frustrating, unscientific and far too mystical.

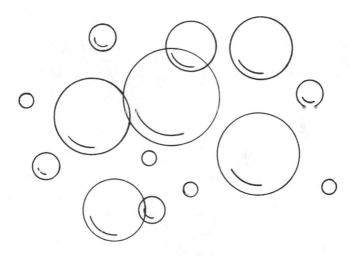

Philosophy of Mind is a complex subject with its arguments and jargon. Philosophers of mind can be dual aspect monists, occasionalists, epiphenomenalists, materialists, functionalists, behaviourists, cognitivists, or even "don't knows". The directions that these philosophers have taken and the kinds of problems they debate are almost all a direct result of Descartes' original discovery of the Cogito and his own thoughts about it. The various debates about mind may sound like eccentric philosophers' games at times, but they go to the heart of how we human beings conceive of ourselves and how we think we fit into the world around us. Descartes may not have always produced very satisfactory answers to the problems he raised – but he set the agenda.

Open to Criticism

Meditations on First Philosophy, published in 1641 in Latin, as we have just seen, shows Descartes engaged in daily personal and private meditations on how to find a wholly certain and reliable basis for human knowledge. **Meditations** is more exploratory than doctrinal. Descartes insisted that his book was to be regarded as an open text to be shared with the reader.

I would not urge anyone to read this book except those who are able and willing to meditate seriously along with me ...

In this spirit of openness, Descartes corresponded with many of his contemporaries who all had different views of the human mind. Their criticisms of the dualist doctrine and his replies to them were both published in a section of **Meditations** called *Objections and Replies*.

Philosophers like **Thomas Hobbes** (1588-1679), **Pierre Gassendi** (1592-1655) and **Marin Mersenne** (1588-1648) criticized Descartes for various reasons, but he was always confident that his ideas were valid.

I shall be glad if people make the strongest objections they can, for I hope that in consequence the truth will stand out all the better.

The Mind and Body Problem

The problem with Cartesian dualism is still that mental and physical worlds seem so very different.

The physical world consists of material objects which exist in space and time and obey certain laws that can be established by physics.

The mental world is populated with thoughts which seem to be outside of space and time and which are subjective, private and unique to each individual.

How does mind operate on matter and matter on mind? Most philosophers produced their own unique monist or dualist theories to answer these problems. The mind-body problem certainly exercised the minds of most 17th century philosophers very greatly. They emerged with different solutions which usually seem more theological than philosophical.

Some Odd Answers

One utterly odd dualist theory is **Occasionalism**, popularized by **Nicolas Malebranche** (1638-1715). He explains how mind and matter interact simply by denying that they do so.

Mental thoughts and physical actions just coincide, they don't **cause** one another.

The solution of **Benedictus de Spinoza** (1632-77) is equally strange. Spinoza abandoned the "two substance" view of Descartes for a monist or "one substance" view. The **Double Aspect Theory** maintains that mental and physical events are merely different aspects of the same substance which, it turns out, is God.

God is the essence or nature of everything that exists.

And **that** is why mind and body exist in a constant state of coordination.

G.W. Leibniz (1646-1716) went for a variation on Malebranche's idea, sometimes called **Psychophysical Parallelism**. He explains it like this. Imagine there are two clocks that have been synchronized to tell the same time. It might *look* as if one causes the other to tell the same time, but both clocks are wholly separate. The same is true for minds and bodies that always seem to correlate.

Occasionalism suggests an answer, but one that seems to rely on a God who is unnecessarily busy. Leibniz submits that God establishes a harmony between the two from day one, and then ceases to interfere.

Epiphenomenalism is an equally odd version of dualism. It suggests that any interaction is all one way. Physical events in the body do cause mental events, but mental events never cause physical ones.

My mind is merely a convenient and perhaps comforting "epiphenomenon". It's an odd view, because it means that human beings have no such thing as free-will, and that causation can operate in one direction only.

How Did Brains Evolve Minds?

From the very start, many scientists and philosophers have worried about Descartes' model of the mind because of its metaphysical assumptions. Human beings are primates that have evolved over time. Many modern scientists find it difficult to accept that human beings are the only species that possesses non-physical minds or that such odd spiritual entities could have evolved from physical beginnings.

Where could minds have come from?

You could maintain that all life forms **do** possess souls or minds to some degree, although this seems hard to accept when you think about some lower life forms, such as spiders.

The 20th century has witnessed the success of a materialist science that assumes that all things **can** be explained in terms of physical entities and forces, but irritatingly, minds don't seem to be investigable in that sort of way.

Neuroscientists are happy with talk about "firing synapses" in the brain, but shuffle about uneasily when they try to explain how non-physical thoughts cause physical actions.

What is Consciousness?

Consciousness itself **should be** a biological phenomenon. We have evolved as beings with this attribute. And yet, it seems very different from some of our other physical processes, like growth and digestion. It is different because of its subjectivity and uniqueness.

This is why I said there was only one kind of "extended substance", but as many "mental substances" as there are individual human beings.

Nevertheless, it seems likely that physical brain processes cause consciousness to exist, although the how and where of it remain very mysterious. It's also not wholly clear why human beings need consciousness in the first place. Some scientists now believe that science may be able to explain consciousness by turning to something like **quantum theory** where the usual laws of causality dissolve.

Aspects of Consciousness

So, the Cogito is a major problem. It certainly doesn't seem to be as "clear and distinct" as Descartes thought. For most people, consciousness is like a kind of "inner light" that determines "what it is like to be me". Other features seem to be those of Unity, Intentionality, Central and Peripheral ability, an aptitude for *gestalt* perception, and a need for familiarity. When we are conscious, we experience everything at the same time in a **unified** manner.

... the breathing of the dog by the fire, the sound of a radio in the kitchen, as well as the words on the page of a book.

Consciousness also usually has content or **intentionality** – it is directed at something.

> Normally, we are anxious **about** something rather than just "being anxious".

> We are usually conscious about different things on **different levels of awareness.**

> You may be very aware of the book you're reading, but only semi-aware of the dog's breathing and the radio in the kitchen.

When we look up from a book and look at a room, we grasp it **as a whole** and not as disconnected bits of wall and furniture. We know what we are looking at, because we are **familiar** with the kinds of categories that things like chairs and wallpaper fit into.

Brains not Minds

So consciousness is varied in its achievements – but is it a Cartesian non-physical entity or something more mundanely corporeal? Most neuroscientists claim that all mental events can be explained in physical terms – usually by using the term "brain" and avoiding the awkward "mind" word. They resort to a kind of **monism** that they can live with.

By reducing all mental processes to physical events, they become less worryingly metaphysical and subject to physical laws like everything else.

But, however hard they try to do this, somehow there are lots of aspects of human feelings, beliefs and pains that don't seem to be explicable in this reductive way. Human beings seem to be relentlessly dualist in the ways that they think about themselves. Materialists might claim to be explaining what mind and thoughts are, when perhaps what they are **really** trying to do is explain awkward things like consciousness out of existence.

Behaviourists

The Behaviourist way out of the "mind dilemma" is virtually to deny the existence of mind altogether.

All descriptions of private mental experiences should be "translated" into accounts of public dispositions and tendencies.

"Being sad" means crying and moaning. It is not some private mental event. There is no "ghost in the machine", as the Behaviourist philosopher **Gilbert Ryle** (1900-76) once said. Behaviourists believe that to envisage human beings as "souls in bodies" is a kind of category mistake – rather as if we were to confuse "Thursdays" with "tables".

Problems with Behaviourism

But if this Behaviourist account of human beings were true, there could be no difference between someone *being* sad and someone *pretending* to be sad. Someone who was paralyzed and could not exhibit behaviour would presumably have no mental life. Behaviourists also ignore **qualia** – what it actually *feels like* to be in a particular state of mind.

> It also seems odd to suggest that we acquire beliefs somehow by observing our own behaviour.

> And mental beliefs are quite clearly often the cause of behaviour.

For behaviourists this just isn't possible, because belief and behaviour are synonymous. The Behaviourist model just isn't convincing. A feeling of pain is one thing; but the behaviour we associate with pain is something quite different.

Physicalists

Physicalist or **Mind/Brain Identity theorists** believe that mental
and physical events are the same. To think about Descartes growing
vegetables is no more than a particular state of the brain. To believe
that "mind" and "brain" are different and to talk about them differently
is rather like someone who talks about "lightning" and "electrical
discharges", believing that they are different things when they are
the same.

Although the language we use
to talk about minds seems very
different from the language we
use to talk about brains, in
reality we are talking about
the same thing.

In principle, a neuroscientist could eventually give a detailed account of
the brain state that is my thought about Descartes eating a carrot as
"an activity occurring in sector 1374B of the subject's brain".

Problems

The problem with this explanation lies in the words "in principle". So far, neuroscientists are nowhere near having this kind of detailed knowledge of where thoughts occur in the brain, even though we as individuals all have clear and immediate access to our own thoughts. Thoughts and brain processes just don't seem to be the same sorts of thing at all.

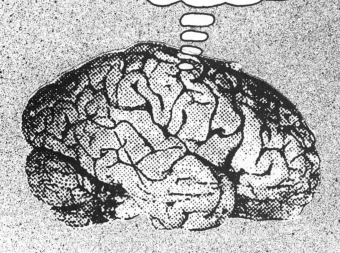

Thoughts don't exist in a particular location in the way that brain states presumably do. And thoughts seem to be "about" something in a way that brain states aren't.

Also, individual thoughts just don't seem to be divisible or measurable in the way that brain states presumably would be, as physical phenomena.

When we experience our own feelings, like those of pain and desire (those **qualia** again!), they are unique to us.

Token Identity theory tries to get around some of these problems by suggesting that individual thoughts may be tokens (individual examples) of a type (an identical species of brain state). This means that two totally identical human beings could have identical brains in which were identical brain states, and yet still be having utterly different thoughts. If that is the case, then the relationship between the physical and the mental still remains wholly mysterious and bizarre.

Functionalism

Functionalism is the most recent attempt to resolve the dilemma of what consciousness and thoughts are, and how they can be explained. Functionalism exploits a now familiar computer analogy. Human thoughts are like software processed by the hardware – the human brain.

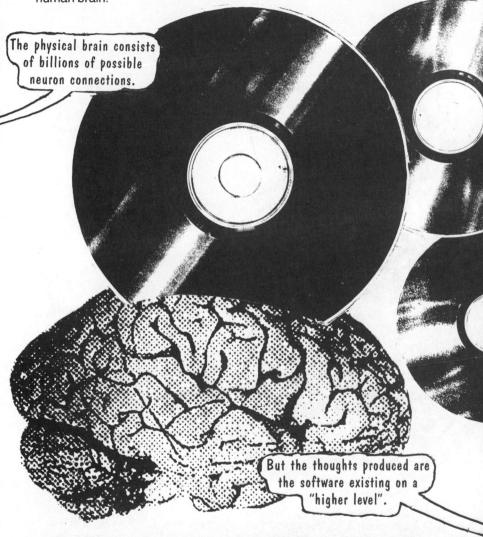

The physical brain consists of billions of possible neuron connections.

But the thoughts produced are the software existing on a "higher level".

It is the mental software that is crucial – not the physical brain activity. Thoughts, like software, don't have a spatial location. To ask where thoughts "exist" is like asking where Mozart's Requiem "exists".

Functionalists are still materialists, but they expand what is normally regarded as "material" or "physical" by talking about "structures" or "systems" rather than matter. They stress how "exist" doesn't have to mean the same as "tangible" or "visible". Thoughts and consciousness exist on a kind of higher and more conceptual level – just like computer software "exists". Mental states are mental because of their causal relations.

A clock can still be a clock, whether it is made of metal springs or electrical impulses.

It's what the clock **does** and not what it is **made of** that defines it.

The same is true of thoughts and consciousness. Both do exist in the human brain, but could do so equally well in some other kinds of alien being or sophisticated machine wired up quite differently to us. It's the software, not the hardware that determines thought.

Problems

It all sounds sensible enough, but at the end of the day, Functionalists still maintain that something like a human belief is eventually reducible to a bunch of firing neurons that produce the correct sort of causal relations. Mental states are functional states and functional states are physical states.

This attempt to push the meanings of "material" and "physical" as far as they can go is the most recent attempt to escape from the mysticism of dualism and the obvious problems of behaviourism and physicalism.

Humans and Computers

Functionalism also raises the issue of whether computers can really *think* and be *conscious* as well. If it's the software that produces consciousness, and the nature of the physical hardware involved is irrelevant, then presumably computers could eventually become conscious. The possibility of thinking machines was an idea that interested Descartes. He thought that it might well be possible to build an automaton that looked human, and seemed, on the surface, to think and use language like we do.

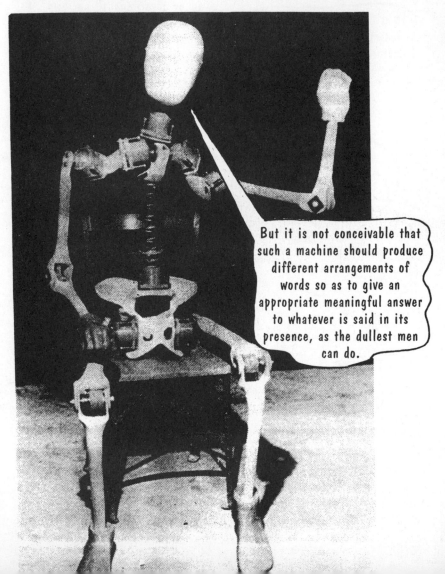

But it is not conceivable that such a machine should produce different arrangements of words so as to give an appropriate meaningful answer to whatever is said in its presence, as the dullest men can do.

Can Computers Understand?

Descartes seems to have anticipated many of the current debates in the 20th century about artificial intelligence. He would probably have agreed with the philosopher **John Searle** (b. 1932) who argues that a computer can manipulate data efficiently but can never *understand* it in the way that human beings do.

Human consciousness just isn't a digital or computational phenomenon.

A computer is rather similar to a non-Chinese speaking man locked in a room who receives, rearranges and then posts a whole series of Chinese characters according to a set of rules.

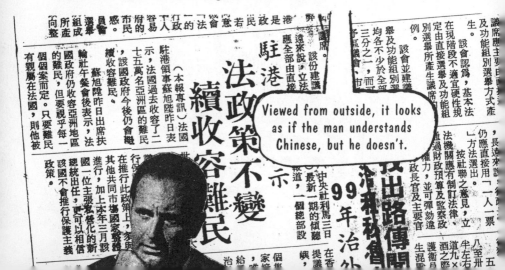

Viewed from outside, it looks as if the man understands Chinese, but he doesn't.

So computers may *look* as if they understand thoughts and ideas, but they don't. This suggests that, although the computer analogy and the functionalist theory may provide us with new ways of escaping from the dualist dilemma, they may still not tell us the whole story about minds and thoughts and how they relate to physical brains.

And even if we **could** build a computer that eventually somehow became conscious, it still wouldn't **explain** what consciousness is ...

It certainly seems odd to believe that a machine, however cleverly wired up with its own circuits firing away, could ever experience pain in the inner, subjective and intensely unpleasant way that we human beings do. Human beings are different from everything else in the world precisely because of our *first person* perspective.

We are part of the physical world, but perhaps we aren't reducible to it in the sort of "third person" perspective that materialism and science adopt.

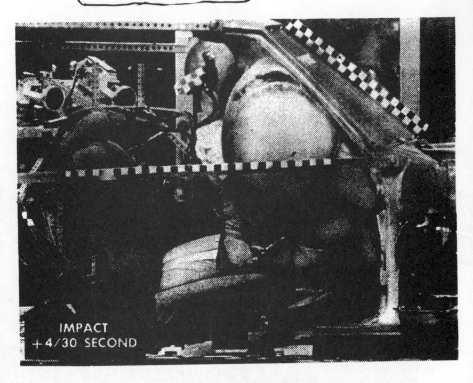

IMPACT
+4/30 SECOND

The phenomena of consciousness and thought at present seem to be beyond the grasp of both philosophers and scientists. Modern theories of mind often seem more like attempts to side-step both as problems, perhaps because they are ultimately unsolvable. The last laugh may still lie with René Descartes. His Cogito is as mysterious a thing as it ever was.

The Principles

In 1643, Descartes began corresponding with Princess Elizabeth of Bohemia, who was herself living in exile in Holland. She was an unusually intelligent 24-year-old and challenged Descartes with many disturbing questions about his views on the relationships between mind and body, reason, the passions and morality.

In 1644, Descartes published his last great work, **Principles of Philosophy**, in which he gave accounts of metaphysics, physics and the physical universe.

I hope my work will be a substitute textbook for all of the outdated Aristotle still studied in the universities.

René Descartes

PRINCIPLES OF PHILOSOPHY *

He vigorously rejected much of Aristotle's teleological doctrine (in which everything is supposed to have a final cause for its existence), and still tentatively suggested that it was the earth that moved around the sun and not the other way around.

Retirement

Descartes subsequently supervised French translations of his **Meditations** and **Principles** from their original Latin. (Latin was still used as the universal language of scholarship throughout Europe.) He spent the rest of his life in the Netherlands countryside, eating vegetables from his own garden and corresponding with friends.

To be happy, one must live in seclusion.
— Ovid.

In 1648, a young scholar called Frans Burman visited the 52-year-old philosopher and wrote down an account of all the conversations he had with Descartes.

The old philosopher now wanted to retreat from the world of constant academic squabbling and the stream of condemnations which came from both Protestant and Catholic theologians.

They have all mastered the art of denigration.

In 1649, he wrote his last work, **The Passions of the Soul**, a book on ethics and the good life.

Descartes and Ethics

Perhaps wisely, Descartes has surprisingly little to say about ethics or politics in his philosophical works. But he was interested in the sort of life that we need to lead if we are to be happy and fulfilled. He was a great believer in science, which he thought would benefit human beings in the long run by enabling them both to be healthier and to live longer.

Like the Stoic philosophers, I think that human beings would be wiser and happier if they used reason to guide and control their instincts and passions.

...MY HEART WAS ON FIRE WITH DESIRE FOR YOU...

In **Passions of the Soul**, he maintains that passions and emotions like love, desire, hatred and joy, are experiences which arise in the soul but are caused by the body.

This means that we must train ourselves to subdue these merely physiological events by exerting our will-power. If we could do this, then our lives would never be confused, and our knowledge would increase rapidly.

It sounds very dull. Perhaps it's an over-optimistic vision of what human beings are like and what they can achieve. In the centuries that have passed since Descartes started to think, human beings have seemed unable to control their violent and destructive passions. Furthermore, they have employed reason and science as much to serve these passions as to control them.

Invitation to England?

Descartes almost made a journey to England in 1640 at the invitation of Sir Charles Cavendish. One legend says that he paid a brief visit in 1641, but this seems very unlikely. He seems to have gone off the idea of visiting England.

Invitation to Sweden

Descartes had been corresponding with Queen Christina of Sweden for several years. In 1649, perhaps with a sense of relief, he accepted an invitation to be her philosophy tutor. Queen Christina was an eccentric blue-stocking.

She refuses traditional women's clothing and wears flat shoes.

She was also an excellent horse-rider and spoke six languages. She had a rather masculine voice and studied at least six hours every day.

All Frenchmen Dance ...

Almost immediately after he arrived, the Queen asked him to dance in a ballet! Descartes sensibly refused.

Lessons at 5 A.M.

Descartes had reservations about going to a land of "bears, rocks and ice".

It was a bitterly cold winter. Descartes had to break the late-rising habits of a lifetime and walk to the palace every morning in the dark.

He died of pneumonia in 1650, after only a few months in Sweden. His dying words were reported as: *"Ça mon âme; il faut partir."* Thirteen years later his works were banned by the Roman Catholic Church and put on the Index of Forbidden Books.

He had very little interest in money. "He was more curious to understand and explain the metals than to amass them." (Baillet) When he died he was relatively poor.

Descartes' letters only just survived his death. He took most of them to Sweden with him. After his funeral, they were returned to Paris by boat. But the boat sank before it reached its destination and hundreds of his letters stayed underwater for three days.

This made me realise that there must be a general science... and that this science should be termed "universal mathematics."

...I urge... read this book... who are able and... meditate seriously along... me, because, quite fran...

Fortunately, most of them were recovered, hung up to dry and found to be still legible, if in a very confused and disordered state.

Descartes' Legacy

Descartes is often called the father of modern philosophy, for very good reasons. The questions he asks will remain interesting as long as there are thinking beings in existence.

I recognized that radically different natural phenomena could all be shown to obey a few fundamental rules which could be expressed mathematically.

If there had been no Descartes, there could have been no Stephen Hawking.

Descartes helped to produce our modern age, with its new ways of thinking about knowledge, in which magic and mysticism have been replaced by scientific and technological systems of thought and control.

After Descartes, science became more systematized and its content and methodologies universally agreed upon. So Descartes is partly responsible for these relatively new ways of thinking we now call "scientific", which gradually emerged in the 17th century and which contributed to make the world we live in today the way it is.

And although Descartes' universe is materialist, cold and geometric, we ourselves remain non-physical and spiritual.

The Thinking Individual

The lasting image of Descartes will probably always be that of the young man sitting out the Bavarian winter in his warm room, determined to discover a new body of knowledge by thinking private thoughts.

It sounds reasonable enough. But most modern philosophers now believe that his great project is fundamentally flawed.

The Postmodern Mind

Not many psychologists or philosophers now accept the Cartesian model of the mind as something "transparent" and so "open to inspection" by us.

We are social animals and we think with a shared public language – something easy to forget when we sit down and think in isolation.

The philosopher **Ludwig Wittgenstein** (1889-1951) spent much of his time demolishing this Cartesian model of the mind and Cartesian doubt by revealing how both are incoherent.

I^N the beginning

It is impossible for us to doubt the existence of an external world whose very language composes all our sceptical thoughts.

Some postmodern psychoanalysts, like **Jacques Lacan** (1901-81), believe that our common belief in a private individual self may itself be a convenient illusion.

was the Word,

Language is prior to any individual. So, if our minds are essentially linguistic, then our human identity is undeniably social.

It's much harder to sit down and think private thoughts than Descartes realized. And it's not wholly clear who is the "**who**" that is having these thoughts.

Trying to give an explanation of consciousness may well be as impossible a task as solving what was around before the "Big Bang" created the universe.

"How do we really think?"

Descartes' explanation of what it is to think and perceive is also problematic. At bottom his explanation is tautological. He ascribes to some internal "homunculus" or little man the psychological phenomena he is investigating in the first place, so nothing really gets explained.

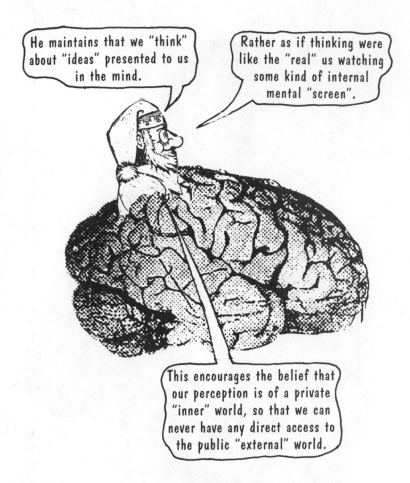

He maintains that we "think" about "ideas" presented to us in the mind.

Rather as if thinking were like the "real" us watching some kind of internal mental "screen".

This encourages the belief that our perception is of a private "inner" world, so that we can never have any direct access to the public "external" world.

Most psychologists now maintain that our experience of the world is far more direct and immediate than this model implies. They would also stress how active and creative perception is – perceiving is more like the brain instantaneously writing a novel, rather than a little man going to the movies.

Knowledge and Certainty

Descartes' project of establishing a new systematic body of certain scientific knowledge derived from private thoughts and expressed in mathematical form also seems to be an illusion.

David Hume (1711-76)

Karl Popper (1902-94)

Twentieth-century scientists are usually aware that their work must always be regarded as only conjectural probability and that there is no such thing as the sort of certain scientific truth that Descartes thought the mind could acquire.

The Postmodern Condition

Other recent philosophers like **Paul Feyerabend** (1924-94) and **Michel Foucault** (1926-84) stress how scientific knowledge is as much a cultural and political phenomenon as other kinds of knowledge.

So, Descartes may have been wrong to believe that we can ever acquire certain and secure scientific knowledge.

Nowadays, it's the Descartes who **doubts** who seems more like our contemporary.

What was, for him, merely a temporary strategy, now seems to us more like a fundamental truth about the human condition.

The universal scepticism that is postmodernism stems from another invisible demon altogether – the loss of faith in the ability of language to refer to anything other than itself. But that's another story …

niversal scepticism that is postmodernism ste

le demon altogether – the loss of faith in the a

o anything other than itself. But that's another

m that is postmodernis

ther – the loss of faith i

han itself. But that's ar

that is post

Further Reading

One of the best features of Descartes' philosophy is the readability of his major philosophical works – something which can rarely be said about much 20th century philosophy. Descartes' prose is vivid, clear and lively. He encourages the reader to share in the workings of his very active mind. He presents his philosophy as autobiographical and personal intellectual adventures, and not as academic treatises. So, reading the man, as well as his critics, is a worthwhile experience.

A good anthology of Descartes' writings can be found in **Descartes' Philosophical Writings**, ed. Anscombe and Geach (Nelson University Paperbacks, 1970). It contains **Discourse on the Method** and **Meditations**, together with **Objections and Replies** and various letters and extracts from other works.

The translation of Descartes' works used by this author is the two-volume **The Philosophical Writings of Descartes**, translated by Cottingham, Stoothoff and Murdoch (Cambridge University Press, 1985).

The best introduction to Descartes' philosophy is probably to be found in **Descartes** by John Cottingham (Blackwell, 1986). Cottingham's book **Rationalism** (Paladin Granada, 1984) is also very accessible and useful.

There are many other useful critical works on Descartes.

D.M. Clarke, **Descartes' Philosophy of Science** (Manchester University Press, 1982).
E.M. Curley, **Descartes Against the Sceptics** (Blackwell, 1978).
A. Kenny, **Descartes** (Random House, New York, 1968).
Jonathan Rée, **Descartes** (Allen Lane, 1974).
B. Williams, **Descartes, The Project of Pure Enquiry** (Penguin, 1978).

There are many books on the Philosophy of Mathematics. Here are a few.

John D. Barrow, **Pi in the Sky** (Clarendon Press, 1992).
Carl Boyer, **A History of Mathematics** (Wiley, 1995).
Davis and Hersh, **The Mathematical Experience** (Penguin, 1983), and **Descartes' Dream** (Penguin, 1988).
Robert Osserman, **Poetry of the Universe** (Weidenfeld, 1995).
Ian Stewart, **Nature's Numbers** (Weidenfeld & Nicholson, 1995).

Consciousness and the Philosophy of Mind books are published in alarming numbers. Here are a few recent ones.

Francis Crick, **The Astonishing Hypothesis: The Scientific Search for The Soul** (Simon & Schuster, 1994).
Daniel C. Dennet, **Kinds of Minds: Towards an Understanding of Consciousness** (Weidenfeld & Nicholson, 1996).
Owen Flanagan, **Consciousness Reconsidered** (MIT, 1995).
Richard Gregory (ed.), **The Oxford Companion to the Mind** (Oxford University Press, 1987).
David Hodgson, **The Mind Matters: Consciousness and Choice in a Quantum World** (Oxford University Press, 1995).
Darryl Reaney, **Music of the Mind: An Adventure into Consciousness** (Souvenir, 1995).

The Philosophy of Science is a daunting subject, but there are two excellent introductory books on the subject.

A.F. Chalmers, **What is this thing called Science?** (Open University Press, 1980).
Anthony O'Hear, **An Introduction to the Philosophy of Science** (Oxford University Press, 1990).

And for the doubters: Christopher Hookway, **Scepticism** (Routledge, 1990).

Acknowledgements

The author of **Introducing Descartes** would like to express his thanks to Chris Garratt for helping to make a sometimes difficult book into a more amusing and accessible one. He also owes a large debt to his extremely experienced editor, Richard Appignanesi.

Layout assistants

Sophie Garratt
Timothy Garratt

ndex

The Authors

Dave Robinson has taught philosophy to students for many years. He has recently written and illustrated *Leading Questions*, a book about postmodernist literary theory. He is also the author of *Introducing Ethics* and *Introducing Philosophy*.

Chris Garratt is the illustrator of the BIFF cartoon strip in *The Guardian*. He is also the illustrator of *Introducing Ethics*, *Introducing Postmodernism* and *Keynes for Beginners*.